Why I'd Rather Date My Dog

MUSINGS FOR SAVVY SINGLES

Why I'd Rather Date My Dog

■ MUSINGS FOR SAVVY SINGLES ■

By Nancy Furstinger

Illustrated by Jamey Christoph

BOWTIE
PRESS®

A Division of BowTie, Inc.®
Irvine, California

Karla Austin, *Business Operations Manager*
Nick Clemente, *Special Consultant*
Barbara Kimmel, *Managing Editor*
Jessica Knott, *Production Supervisor*
Amy Stirnkorb, *Designer*

Copyright © 2007 by Nancy Furstinger
Illustrations © 2007 by Jamey Christoph

All rights reserved. No part of this book may be reproduced, stored in
a retrieval system, or transmitted in any form or by any means, elec-
tronic, mechanical, photocopying, recording, or otherwise, without
the prior written permission of BowTie Press®, except for the inclusion
of brief quotations in an acknowledged review.

Library of Congress Cataloging-in-Publication Data

Furstinger, Nancy.
  Why I'd rather date my dog : musings for savvy singles /
by Nancy Furstinger ; illustrations by Jamey Christoph.
      p. cm.
  ISBN-13: 978-1-933958-04-0
  ISBN-10: 1-933958-04-9
   1.   Dating (Social customs)—Anecdotes. 2.   Dogs—Behavior—
Anecdotes. I. Title.

  HQ801.F885 2007
  306.81'5—dc22

                                            2006100209

BowTie Press®
A Division of BowTie, Inc.
3 Burroughs
Irvine, California 92618

16 15 14 13 12 11 10 09 08 07   1 2 3 4 5 6 7 8 9 10

Dedication

For Sherrie Duncan, my best pal
since junior high.
Whenever I count my blessings,
I count you twice.

Contents

Introduction

After a disastrous date, who hasn't regretted not spending the time with his or her dog instead? Bachelors and bachelorettes know that when romance has gone to the dogs, their pooches can be counted on to provide a daily dose of love.

I know that my debonair Rottweiler mix, Splash Kisser, is generous with his affections. His love is absolute, and he shares his passion with everyone he encounters. Splash likes to play Cupid for his friends of many species (he found his own match, Labrador Retriever Lacy Whirly-gig, through http://www.Petfinder.com).

This marvelous mutt is also the barometer of my love interests—his instincts are always on target. He wants to steer me to the good ones!

Splash's idea of a perfect date—hiking to a mountain-top and splashing in a lake, followed by pizza, pistachio ice cream, and a wildlife documentary—matches mine. If I could find a man like Splash, I'd romance him for the rest of my life!

When I revealed to friends (male and female, teens to seniors, gay and straight) my list of reasons why I'd rather date my dog, their enthusiasm for my ideas spread like chicken pox through a kindergarten class. Everyone in

the dog-eat-dog dating scene seemed to prefer relating to their canine companions to relating to their human counterparts.

"The more I see of men, the more I admire dogs," French revolutionary Jeanne-Marie Roland wrote in the 1700s. She could have penned these words today (using more gender-neutral language) to describe exasperating dating experiences.

Dating in the twenty-first century offers more options for connecting with a special breed of person—along with more chances to meet people who are "dogs" in the derogatory sense. Besides the traditional methods of meeting that special someone, Internet dating sites have become increasingly popular—and specialized. Sites catering to single pet lovers proliferate, which proves there is no shortage of people searching for puppy love. Some sites also give a double bang for your buck, guaranteeing that both you and your pet will receive virtual kisses from prospective dates and their pets. If you match, you can all share smooches with pooches in person!

Or you may prefer to meet your match in a more traditional fashion—escorted by your dog, of course! Studies have shown that people who are accompanied by pooches on their outings are three times more likely to meet someone than are those who are solo. Parks, beaches, dog runs, and doggy happy hours at outdoor cafés are all hot spots where your dog can help you sniff out a date.

All this animal magnetism can either create sparks or go haywire. Dating ranks high on the stress scale for the 90 million Americans who are single. And dog lovers looking for a match appreciate a touch of humor to help diffuse dating anxiety.

The following quips about why dogs make the best dates will, I hope, provide an entertaining oasis in the stressful dating scene.

The Canine Advantage

Dogs never Google you before
a first date. They prefer to dig up the dirt
in their own backyards.

Dogs don't gossip.
They wag their tails rather
than their tongues.

Dogs never snoop inside your wallet or medicine chest.
They check you out with a sniff, not a detective.

Cyberspace dating is really blind dating
in the new millennium. And who better to accompany
you on a blind date than a dog?

A dog with Peter Pan syndrome—who never grows up—is appealing; his human counterpart is exasperating!

A date with a canine bitch is guaranteed not to be a romantic catastrophe.

Dogs yell, "Yahoo!" each time they see you.
Whether you've been gone five minutes or five days,
your arrival is always a reason for celebration.

If you're late, your dog is more excited than ever
to greet you. And your dog doesn't expect you
to call first to explain your tardiness.

With dogs, playing with balls doesn't
conjure up fears of STDs.

Canine females in heat can be fixed.
And you can prove that you love male dogs
by castrating them.

When a dog is interested in you, the only things
he pricks up are his ears and tail.

Dogs don't play mind games. They are honest in their appraisals: if something is acceptable, they'll wag their tails (or butts); if it's not, they'll lift their legs.

Dogs never accidentally call you by an old flame's name. And if you unintentionally call your dog by another dog's name, she will forgive you.

Dogs have no ulterior motives when they nibble your ear.

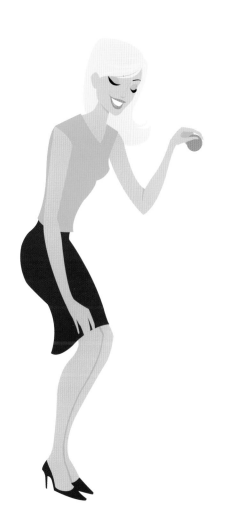

If your dog disappears, just dangle a toy, and he'll be back in an instant.

When a dog's tongue hangs out,
it's for a valid reason.

Dogs can retain their dignity when they
slobber all over you.

Staring and drooling at the object of one's desire is proper behavior for a dog.

A panting dog is not depraved.

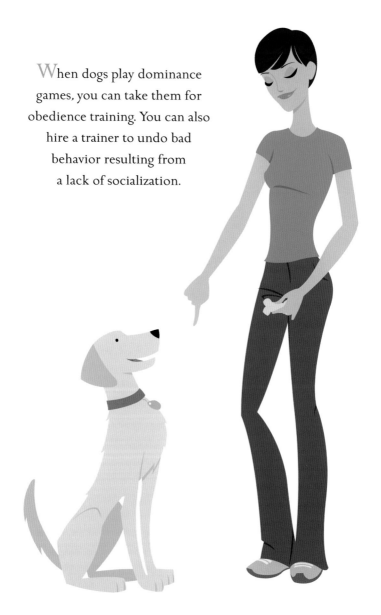

When dogs play dominance games, you can take them for obedience training. You can also hire a trainer to undo bad behavior resulting from a lack of socialization.

When you give the command *no*,
dogs know you don't mean "maybe."

For a dog, being a party animal simply
means wolfing down hot dogs.

Dogs will never require the
"hair of the dog" to cure a hangover.

Dogs don't get jealous when they smell another dog on you.

You can share the affections of two or more dogs at the same time.

Dogs don't demand designer duds and other trinkets as proof of your affection. The only jewelry they need to show off is an ID tag and license.

A dog is flattered when you call him a scamp or a cur.

Dogs never need to ask for directions. They rely on their instincts and keen senses instead of GPS devices.

A dog doesn't mind when you leave
lipstick prints on his collar.

Dogs will never pen some silly doggerel
to try to win your heart.

You can keep a dog on a short leash.
(Don't attempt this with someone you're dating!)

It's a natural situation for dogs
to be "in the doghouse."

Dogs don't demand that you discuss issues
for the umpteenth time.

Dogs never need to examine
the relationship.

Dogs are comfortable and secure
with a routine.

When you require
help, a dog will willingly
come to the rescue.

Dogs are thrilled to meet your
friends and relatives.

Dogs always appear captivated
by your conversation.

Dogs adore attachment.

You'll never wonder whether your
dog is good enough for you. However, you
might question whether you are good
enough for your dog.

Dogs Just Want to Have Fun

Dogs are raring to go anytime, anywhere. Unlike humans, they don't have to be coaxed into an adventure.

Dogs are inventive. When they lack playmates, they'll chase their own tails rather than search for tails to chase.

You can act foolish around your dog, and instead of chewing you out, she will join you.

Dogs beg, but they expect only a biscuit in return.

Dogs are never too tired to fetch—and always believe you look fetching no matter what your appearance.

Petting is interpreted literally by a dog.

Rough play is OK for both the dog and you.

It is socially acceptable to dress your dog
in leather and have him fetch.

Dogs are easy to please—a few belly rubs
and body scratches satisfy any dog.

It's OK if your dog rubs up against your best friend.
It's also OK if your best friend caresses your dog.

Dogs do tricks for treats.

When you stroke a dog,
her ego doesn't get overblown.

Dogs enjoy watching sports on television,
especially if the mascot is a Husky or a Bulldog.

Dogs can be tamed by being trained
to obey commands.

Dogs can be as tough as dewclaws while still
being in touch with their inner puppy.

You *can* teach an old dog new tricks.

You can groom
dogs and dress
them up for special
occasions.

Dogs don't expect you to whip up a gourmet meal. You can impress your dog just by opening a can.

You can rub dogs the wrong way,
and they will be blissful.

Dogs toy with you only
when they want to play.

Dogs always clean their plates and ask for seconds.

Dogs don't expect reservations at the swankiest
spot in town. They're happy to celebrate
special occasions with a doggie bag.

Dogs don't need scotch and water to relax.
They prefer toilet water!

With the right treats, it's easy to get a dog to eat out of your hand.

Dogs love living in the moment, unlike humans, who linger in the past or obsess about the future.

Your dog won't whine if you ask him to be your exercise partner.

Dogs are just as happy hanging out at home
as they are going out on the town.

Dogs don't drag you to parties.
They create their own party every time you
enter the room, and they insist that you are
always the center of attention.

Dogs grasp the significance of a good cuddle.
They always enjoy snuggling with you
for as long as you desire.

Dogs are as obsessed with you as you are with them. It's a compliment when they hound you.

Dogs don't need witty banter to keep you entertained. They're a real howl when you scratch their tickle spots or get them to cock their heads. And they can make you laugh with their contortionist feats as they attempt to scratch unreachable spots!

Dogs don't gab through movies, nor do they give away the ending.

Dogs do everything they can to charm and amuse you.

Dogs joyfully express their affection anywhere
and anytime. They are constantly thrilled to see
you and smother you with kisses.

Dogs are natural born dancers. They instinctively swing their rear ends in time to the tempo.

Dogs bark along with you when you sing.

Dogs howl at all your jokes, even the corny ones. They never give away the punch lines, and they never bore you with shaggy dog stories.

Dogs are always eager to accompany you on a walk.

Dogs love to show off for you—and to show you off.

Going for a joyride is a joyous event for a dog.
He doesn't speed with paws of lead or
engage in backseat driving.

Dogs don't rely on dating Web sites or
self-help books to find someone special.
Dogs naturally attract friends wherever they go.
And if they aren't successful in relationships,
it's usually the human's fault.

You don't have to nag dogs to try new things—
they are always ready and willing.

The
Outer Hound

Faces that resemble a squashed toad
are endearing in dogs.

Dogs never reject you when you gain
five pounds. As long as you have a soft lap
available, they approve of your size.

Wrinkles and a hangdog appearance
are charming on a dog.

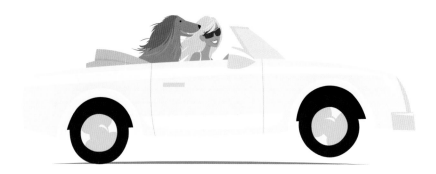

Dogs don't mind if their hair gets mussed
in the breeze when riding
in convertibles.

Hairy ears on a dog are adorable.

Dazzling dogs aren't vain.

Handsome and gorgeous
dogs aren't fazed by homely
human companions.

Dogs don't obsess over the style of their fur and whether there's enough of it.

Hip problems aren't caused
by overindulging in chocolate.

Prior to Valentine's Day, dogs don't drop hints
about mink coats. They know that only creatures
born with fur look glamorous wearing it.

Small dogs do not suffer from
Napoleon complexes.

Dogs adore you more than they adore themselves.
For them, the mirror is just another playmate.

If dogs think you're "a dog," consider yourself a ten.

The aroma of spring mud on a dog is less
overpowering than cloying cologne or
putrid perfume on humans.

If your dog has offensive body odor,
you can give him a bath.

Dogs don't pester you about your
personal appearance.

The Beauty in the Beast

Dogs know that size counts—
the size of the heart, that is.

Dogs never become bored with you.
A dog entering his middle years won't abandon
you for a younger, trophy mistress.

Lack of commitment is
never an issue with dogs.
They are available for you
around the clock, not just
when it's convenient.

Dogs don't cheat on you or take advantage of you.
They are loyal and pledge their lifelong allegiance
to you, saving oodles in therapy bills.

Dogs are always ready to lend an ear—or a paw.

Dogs seduce you with chocolaty eyes
of liquid love and nuzzles from their muzzles—
without giving you whisker burn.

Dogs sniff butts and crotches using less deceit than
most people do when composing personal ads.

You can safely scratch dogs' tickle spots!
When dogs have an itch that needs scratching, they
do not have ulterior motives on their minds.

Dogs who heed the call of the wild and who chase tails
don't regret it in the morning.

Putting out to a dog means he should anticipate getting
food, water, treats, and toys.

Dogs whine only when they need to go outside.

If a dog leans
against you and
begs for caresses,
he's promising you
eternal devotion—
honestly.

Dogs' dispositions don't change according to the time of the month.

Clingy behavior in dogs is expected, not intrusive.

Dogs always wake up with a smile
on their tails.

Dogs are eternally grateful for all
you do for them.

Dogs don't "put on the dog" with snooty airs. What you see is what you get.

Dogs dig to discover buried bones;
they don't dig for gold.

Pet names will not embarrass
your dog in public.

Dogs have never learned how to master
the wolf whistle. They prefer the silent dog whistle!

When dogs sniff you for strange scents,
they are elated to find them.

Dogs will forgive you for playing
with other dogs.

You don't have to hide your IQ from your dog. He doesn't feel threatened by your brainpower.

A dog doesn't get jealous about the previous dogs
in your life. Nor does a dog become resentful
when you pet another dog.

Dogs don't gossip about their previous partners or complain about their exes nonstop.

Rather than yapping about themselves, dogs prefer to listen to you chat about yourself. They are always enthralled by your soliloquies.

Dogs aren't afraid to show you that they can run circles around you.

Dogs always admire and respect you.
They'll frequently brag about you to all of their friends.

Dogs don't lie about their birth dates.
And they don't care that they age seven years
for every human year.

With dogs, you'll never wonder whether
your date needs obedience training.

Dogs aren't into role playing.
They'll instinctively recognize
you as the top dog or alpha
leader of the pack.

Dogs who get collared are suiting up
for exercise. Potential dates who get collared
will be lining up for their mug shots.

A dog will never stand you up—
and will usually respond to your calls.

Dogs find everything you do
fascinating and are unrestrained in their admiration.
Plus, they're always emotionally available.

There are multitudes of wonderful dogs waiting
to be discovered online and in the classifieds.
It's a safe bet you can find your soul mate in either spot.
However, it's a big gamble to play the dating game
with virtual human strangers who advertise
their single status in these same spots.

Dogs don't resort to sneaky stalking. They are candid about their idolization.

When they look you in the eye, dogs never lie. You can always tell exactly what they are thinking.

Dogs never fake personality traits
to prolong a relationship.

Faithfulness and fidelity are inherent traits
in a dog, not foreign words.

You're always number one with your dog.

Dogs never betray your deepest secrets.
You can reveal everything about your past,
and it won't breed trouble.

To a dog, pet peeves seem illogical.

Princess

Dogs often are worthy of being worshipped.

When you judge dogs,
they never resent it.

Dogs live in the moment. They don't waste energy feeling guilty about past fiascos.

Dogs prefer to bury grudges.

Dogs actually act remorseful when they've done something wrong.

Dogs never withhold their affections or give you the silent treatment when they are angry. They are incapable of playing these types of games.

Dogs are direct about what they desire.
They don't expect you to read their minds.

Dogs successfully communicate without uttering
a single word. Plus, they have great eye contact!

A dog is naturally protective and guards
you using instincts honed during thousands
of years on duty. Some dates don't protect you
when the mud is being flung.

Dogs make modest heroes and heroines,
expecting only a pat on the head as a reward.

You can assess dogs' personalities
by their names. Those named Fido are faithful.
If a dog is named Rover, beware! Too bad we
can't use the same tactics to discover
if someone's name is Mud.

Dogs will always stick by you.
They are bonded to you like Krazy Glue.

Dogs are
irresistible
even when
they're
naughty.

Remember, puppy love lasts forever with a dog!

Epilogue:
The Tail End

The quips in this book are all meant to be taken "tongue in jowl," but there is a related topic that is exceptionally serious: pet adoption. If you are searching for that special someone who is loving and loyal and enjoys long walks in the rain, check your local animal shelter or rescue group.

Here, you'll discover dogs of every imaginable description just waiting for a new leash on life. Between 25 and 30 percent of dogs entering shelters across the country are purebreds. The remainder are mixed breeds—commonly called mutts or mongrels. If you're nuts about mutts, you'll agree that there is nothing common about these personable pooches!

Tragically, not all adoptable dogs find the forever homes they deserve. With seven puppies and kittens born for every one human, there are simply not enough homes to go around. Each year, approximately 61 percent of dogs entering shelters across the country will be euthanized, some 6 to 8 million potential pets.

Consider that each time you adopt a dog you will save two lives—the life of your new pet and the life of another rescue animal that will take over the space formerly occupied by your dog. To save additional lives, help prevent the pet overpopulation problem by neutering your male or spaying your female dog.

If you can't make a lifetime commitment to a pet, consider opening up your heart and home to a foster pet as he awaits his forever home. And you can volunteer your time, talents, and resources to your local animal shelter or rescue group.

Love on a leash is waiting to nuzzle its way into your heart. You may not depart the dating scene because you adopted a pet, but you may find that there are many times when you'd rather date your dog. And you'll certainly never complain about spending Saturday nights at home with your canine companion.